D0415297

THE GREAT BRITISH
STREET PARTY
COOKBOOK

BY NANCY LAMBERT

PUBLISHING PLC

Published by Top That! Publishing plc
Tide Mill Way, Woodbridge, Suffolk, IP12 IAP, UK
www.topthatpublishing.com
Copyright © 2012 Top That! Publishing plc
All rights reserved.

CONTENTS

INTRODUCTION

Break out the bunting … it's street paaaaarrrrrty time! The guests, music, games and activities are sorted, so now it's time to plan the food! First, get organised – have a 'streetmeet' with your neighbours and work out what you are going to cook beforehand. Leave plenty of time so you don't feel rushed and, if you can, cook some of the food the day before and keep it in the fridge!

It's all about having fun at a street party, meeting new friends and sharing good food. Place the food along long tables, loaded with themed decorations, which will make the tables look great and also complement your food. Don't forget the party hats, banners, bunting and streamers too!

This book will provide you with a selection of delicious street party recipes for adults and junior chefs to make together. Double the ingredients if you need to make more for the party, and remember, once you have perfected the recipes, don't be afraid to experiment with the ingredients, fillings and toppings to create and decorate street party treats of your very own!

COOKING TIPS!

• Make sure you use the freshest ingredients available.

• Prepare all the food that you can in advance.

• Throw away any food that has been outside for more than 4 hours, and don't leave food outside for too long before it's eaten.

• Provide lots of drinks for your party guests. See recipes on the following pages for ideas or provide them with smoothies, squash and water – having a street party can be thirsty work!

EQUIPMENT

- To complete the recipes in this book, you will need to use a selection of everyday cooking equipment and utensils, such as mixing bowls, saucepans, a sieve, knives, spoons and forks and a chopping board.

- Of course, you'll need to weigh and measure the ingredients, so you'll need a measuring jug and some kitchen scales too.

- To make some of the recipes in this book, you'll need to use special kitchen equipment. These items (and others that you may not have to hand) are listed at the start of each recipe.

SAFETY & HYGIENE

- Before starting any cooking always wash your hands.

- Cover any cuts with a plaster.

- Wear an apron to protect your clothes.

- Always make sure that all the equipment you use is clean.

- If you need to use a sharp knife to cut up something hard, ask an adult to help you. Always use a chopping board.

- Remember that trays in the oven and pans on the cooker can get very hot. Always ask an adult to turn on the oven and to get things in and out of the oven for you.

- Always ask an adult for help if you are using anything electrical – like an electric whisk.

- Be careful when heating anything in a pan on top of the cooker. Keep the handle turned to one side to avoid accidentally knocking the pan.

- Keep your pets out of the kitchen while cooking.

GETTING STARTED

MEASURING

Use scales to weigh exactly how much of each ingredient you need or use a measuring jug to measure liquids.

MIXING

Use a spoon, balloon whisk or electric hand whisk to mix the ingredients together.

CREATING RECIPES

Once you've made a recipe in this book a few times, think about whether you could make your own version. Don't be afraid to experiment with the recipes to find something you like. Try to think up names for the things you create!

PLEASE NOTE

The temperatures and measurements given in this book are approximate. Use the same measurement conversions throughout your recipe (grams or ounces) to maintain the correct ratios. All of the recipes in this book have been created for adults to make with junior chefs and must not be attempted by an unsupervised child.

Read through each recipe to make sure you've got all the ingredients that you need before you start.

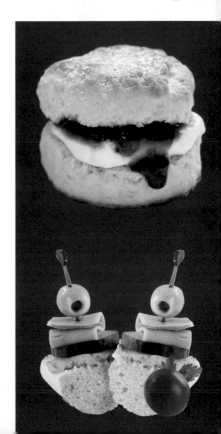

SALAD FACES

Ingredients:

- iceberg lettuce
- lemon, sliced and chopped
- parsley sprigs
- black olives (or grapes)
- tomato, sliced

Wash your iceberg lettuce and lay one large leaf onto a plate.

Ask an adult to slice the lemon, reserving some for later, and place two slices onto the lettuce leaf.

Top with parsley sprigs and black olives for the eyes!

Next, ask an adult to slice the tomato and place it onto the leaf for a smiling mouth.

Then, chop some of the reserved lemon and place around the tomato to make teeth!

Why not use a variety of salad ingredients, such as sweetcorn, cucumber and different types of salad leaves to make different faces?

TOP TIP!
Use the salad face as the centre piece of a party food plate and serve other food at the side.

10

VEGETABLE POTS

Extra equipment:
• colourful pots

Ingredients:
• baby carrots
• 1 cucumber
• 1 red pepper
• 1 celery stick

1 First, wash and prepare the vegetables.

2 Ask an adult to peel the baby carrots.

3 Then chop the cucumber, pepper and celery into slices.

4 Once the vegetables are ready, place them upright in the colourful pots – ready for dipping.

5 Leave a selection of dips out!

TOP TIP! Why not make your own brightly coloured pots using spare card or wrapping paper?

VEGGIE STICKS & DIPS

Ingredients:

For the dips:

Yogurt and Herb:
- 200 g (7 oz) natural yogurt
- 1 teaspoon each dill and mint, chopped

Marie Rose:
- 2 tablespoons mayonnaise
- 2 tablespoons crème fraîche
- 1 tablespoon tomato ketchup
- 1 teaspoon Worcester sauce
- 1 teaspoon lemon juice

For the sticks:
- a selection of fresh vegetables: carrots, celery, cucumber, peppers

For the dips:

 Yogurt and Herb:
Mix the yogurt with the chopped herbs and serve!

 Marie Rose:
Mix all of the ingredients together and serve!

For the veggie sticks:

 First, wash and prepare the vegetables.

 Ask an adult to help you peel and chop up the vegetables into sticks.

 Now, scoop the dips into small bowls and serve with your veggie sticks!

TOP TIP!
Add freshly chopped chives to the marie rose dip for a taste sensation!

HAM & CHEESE PINWHEELS

Extra equipment:
• cling film

Ingredients:
• 260 g (9 oz) cream cheese
• 3 large soft flour tortillas about 24 cm (9 in.) diameter
• 12 thin slices of ham

1 Spread the cream cheese onto each tortilla, followed by four slices of ham.

2 Then roll the tortilla up into a really tight sausage shape. Wrap tightly in cling film and put into the fridge to firm up.

3 Cut the tortilla into small slices about 1 cm (1/2 in.) wide and serve on a platter.

TOP TIP!
The longer you leave the pinwheels in the fridge to chill, the easier they will be to cut.

13

MINI TOMATO BITES

Ingredients:

- 10 small tomatoes
- 1 tin of tuna
- 50 g (2 oz) white rice, cooked
- 25 g (1 oz) peas, cooked
- 25 g (1 oz) red pepper, finely chopped
- basil (optional)

1 First, wash the tomatoes, before placing them on a chopping board. Ask an adult to cut the tops of the tomatoes off. Scoop out the insides with a spoon.

2 Next, mix the tuna, rice, peas and red pepper in a bowl. Fill the tomatoes with the mixture.

3 Top with basil to finish and serve.

TOP TIP!
Try this recipe with hollowed out red peppers – it makes a great main course for a summer barbecue street party.

DELI TOWERS

Extra equipment:
- cocktail sticks

Ingredients:
- 1 French stick or large baguette, cut into chunks
- 1 tub salmon paste
- 1/2 cucumber, sliced
- 100 g (4 oz) cooked ham, sliced
- olives (optional)

1 Starting with the French bread, build up the layers, adding the paste, cucumber slices, ham and olives.

2 Repeat until all of the ingredients have been used up.

3 Make sure the deli towers don't topple over by skewering each one with a cocktail stick.

TOP TIP! Grapes and pineapple chunks make a nice alternative to the olives used in this dish.

15

STAR SANDWICHES

Extra equipment:
- large star-shaped cookie cutter

Ingredients:
- 1 egg
- 2 tablespoons mayonnaise
- butter or margarine, to spread
- 4 slices bread, white or brown
- 2 slices of ham

1. First, make the egg mayonnaise filling. Place the egg in a saucepan half-filled with cold water and ask an adult to bring the water to a boil.

2. Once the water is boiling, turn the heat down and let the egg simmer for about 7 minutes. When the egg has cooked, ask an adult to remove it from the hot water and let it cool.

3. Carefully peel the shell off, then mash the egg using a fork. Put the mashed egg into a bowl and mix together with the mayonnaise. Set aside for later.

4. Next, spread the butter or margarine onto the bread slices.

5. Layer the ham and egg mayonnaise onto one slice of bread, then top with another slice.

6. Repeat with the next two slices of bread.

7. Use the cookie cutter to make star-shaped sandwiches.

TOP TIP!
Don't forget to use other cookie cutters to make different shaped sandwiches!

16

BRILLIANT BREADSTICKS

Extra equipment:
- sieve
- rolling pin
- 2–3 baking trays
- clean tea towel

Ingredients:
- 500 g (1 lb) strong plain flour
- 1 teaspoon salt
- 7 g sachet dried active yeast
- 300 ml (10 fl.oz) water (lukewarm)
- semolina, to sprinkle on the baking trays
- 1 egg, beaten
- 2 tablespoons water
- 1–2 tablespoons sesame seeds

1 Preheat the oven to 200°C / 400°F / gas mark 6.

2 Sift the flour into a bowl and stir in the salt and yeast. Pour 300 ml (10 fl.oz) of lukewarm water into the flour and mix well until it forms a dough.

3 Lightly flour a work surface and knead the dough for about 5–10 minutes, until it is smooth and elastic.

4 Divide the dough in half and roll each piece to about 20 x 30 cm (8 x 12 in.) and then cut widthways into strips about 1 cm (1/2 in.) thick.

5 Sprinkle the baking trays with the semolina, place the strips on top and then cover with a clean tea towel. Leave in a warm place until doubled in size.

6 Mix the egg and 2 tablespoons of water together, then brush the glaze over the strips of dough. Sprinkle with sesame seeds.

7 Bake for 12–15 minutes or until the breadsticks are pale golden in colour.

8 Ask an adult to remove the baking trays from the oven and transfer the sticks onto wire racks to cool.

GARLIC BREAD

Extra equipment:
- foil
- baking tray

Ingredients:
- 3 large garlic cloves, peeled and finely chopped
- 100 g (4 oz) softened butter
- 2 tablespoons flat-leaf parsley
- 1 small baguette

1 Preheat the oven to 180°C / 350°F / gas mark 4.

2 Mix the garlic and butter in a large bowl and then stir in the parsley.

3 Ask an adult to slice the baguette every 2.5 cm (1 in.) along its length (don't cut all the way through) and smear a large amount of the garlic butter into each slice.

4 Then, wrap the baguette in foil.

5 Ask an adult to place the wrapped bread on a baking tray and put into the oven to bake for 10 minutes.

6 Carefully unwrap the bread from the foil and open up.

7 Cut into portions and serve while it's still hot!

TOP TIP!
Sprinkle some grated cheddar cheese on the bread 5 minutes before it's ready!

18

CHICKEN TOWERS

Extra equipment:
• cocktail sticks

Ingredients:
• 100 g (4 oz) pineapple, fresh or tinned, cut into chunks
• 100 g (4 oz) cooked chicken, cut into chunks
• basil leaves
• 2 tomatoes, sliced

1 First, take the pineapple chunks and place the chicken on top.

2 Add the basil on top of the chicken, followed by a slice of tomato. Add another chunk of chicken and finish with a smaller chunk of pineapple.

3 Repeat until all of the ingredients have been used up.

4 Use decorative cocktail sticks to prevent your chicken towers from toppling over.

TOP TIP!
Try cooked gammon for a great variation on this tower recipe.

CRUNCHY COLESLAW

Extra equipment:
• food processor or vegetable shredder

Ingredients:
• 180 g (6 oz) white cabbage
• 1 medium carrot, peeled
• 2 tablespoons mayonnaise

● First, gather together the vegetables that you are going to shred: in this case, the white cabbage and the carrot.

● Set the food processor to the shred setting and place the vegetables inside before blitzing.

● If you haven't got a food processor, shred your vegetables by hand using a vegetable shredder or ask an adult to use a sharp knife.

● Toss the vegetables together in a large bowl.

● Store the coleslaw in the fridge until you are ready to serve and then dress with the mayonnaise.

● Mix well just before serving.

TOP TIP!
Use red cabbage for a more colourful variation of this dish.

POTATO SALAD

Ingredients:

- 675 g (1 lb 8 oz) new potatoes, scrubbed
- 8 tablespoons salad cream
- 1/2 red onion, chopped (optional)
- 50 g (2 oz) spring onions, sliced (optional)
- 1 hard-boiled egg, chopped

1 Put the new potatoes in a saucepan of water, ask an adult to bring to the boil and leave to simmer for 20–25 minutes.

2 When cooked, drain the potatoes, chop into smaller pieces and put them in a large brightly-coloured serving bowl. Leave the potatoes to cool and then add the salad cream, stirring until the potatoes are completely coated.

3 Next, add both types of onion and chopped egg, again stirring until covered.

TOP TIP!
Replace the salad cream with mayonnaise for a less sweet variation of this dish.

MINI JACKET POTATOES

Extra equipment:
• baking tray

Ingredients:
• 12 potatoes
• olive oil
• 200 g (7 oz) cheddar cheese
• topping ingredients of your choice

1 Preheat the oven to 180°C / 350°F / gas mark 4.

2 Lightly grease a large baking tray and ask an adult to place the potatoes on the tray. Rub the potatoes with oil and then bake for 45–50 minutes, or until tender when a skewer is inserted into the centre.

3 Once the potatoes are cooked, preheat the grill.

4 Ask an adult to cut each potato in half. Using a tea towel, hold one potato. Squeeze the base gently to open the top. Repeat with the remaining potatoes.

5 Top with cheddar cheese and any other ingredients you fancy and grill for 2 minutes until the cheese has melted.

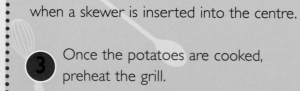

TOP TIP!
Ham, cheese, tomato and sweetcorn make great potato toppings.

MINI SAUSAGE ROLLS

Extra equipment:
- rolling pin
- pastry brush
- baking tray

Ingredients:
- 1 tablespoon butter
- 1 red onion, peeled and finely sliced
- 6 pork sausages
- a handful of breadcrumbs
- 2 tablespoons plain flour
- 250 g (9 oz) ready-made puff pastry
- 1 egg
- a little milk

1 Preheat the oven to 180°C / 350°F / gas mark 4.

2 Melt the butter in a saucepan and add the onions. Cook gently for about 20 minutes until soft. Then, spread out on a plate to cool.

3 Ask an adult to slit the skins of the sausages and pop the meat out. Put the meat in a mixing bowl with the onion and the breadcrumbs, and then scrunch well, with clean hands, to mix together.

4 On a floured work surface, roll the pastry out into a rectangle so it is about 1 cm (1/2 in.) thick. Then, cut it lengthways into two long, even rectangles.

5 Roll the mixture, made in step 3, into sausage shapes with your hands, and lay along the centre of each rectangle.

6 Mix the egg and milk and brush over the pastry. Then, fold one side of the pastry over the filling. Press down with your fingers or the edge of a spoon to seal.

7 Cut the long rolls into the size you want and space them out on a baking tray. Brush with the rest of the egg mix and bake for 25 minutes or until puffed and golden.

TOP TIP!
Pile the sausage rolls on brightly coloured plates!

BITE-SIZED BURGERS

Ingredients:

- 1 kg (2 lb, 2 oz) minced beef
- 1 onion, finely chopped
- 4 tablespoons fine breadcrumbs
- 2 eggs, lightly beaten
- pinch of salt and pepper to season
- 1 teaspoon mustard
- 2 cloves garlic, peeled and crushed

To serve:

- mini burger buns (or bread cut to size)
- salad
- cheese, sliced

1 Preheat the grill / pan / barbecue to a medium heat.

2 Place the minced beef in a large bowl and add the remaining ingredients. Mix it all together, either with your hands or a spoon, until just combined.

3 Wet your hands, and then mould the mixture into burger shapes about 2 cm (1 in.) thick.

4 The burgers can now be cooked either on a griddle pan, non-stick frying pan with a dash of oil, under the grill or on a barbecue. Make sure you preheat the frying pan, griddle pan, grill or barbecue to a medium heat before placing the burgers on top.

5 Cook the burgers for about 4 minutes on each side, turning them once.

6 Serve with mini burger buns, salad and cheese (optional).

TOP TIP!
Why not add some home-made tomato salsa to your burger? Just chop up some fresh tomatoes, red onion, coriander and garlic!

MINI CHICKEN BURGERS

Extra equipment:
• food processor

Ingredients:
• 450 g (1 lb) chicken mince
• 2–3 cloves garlic, peeled and crushed
• 25 g (1 oz) Italian flat leaf parsley
• ½ tsp dried oregano
• ½ tsp dried basil
• ½ lemon, juice only
• salt and pepper
• 6–8 mini burger buns
• salad (optional)

1 In a large bowl, thoroughly combine the chicken mince, garlic, parsley, oregano, basil and lemon juice. Season with salt and pepper. Ask an adult to place the ingredients in a food processor and mix.

2 Once mixed, mould the chicken mixture into about 6–8 patties, about 5 cm (2 in.) in diameter.

3 Ask an adult to heat the oil in a frying pan over a medium heat. Cook the patties for 8–10 minutes until they are browned on each side and cooked through.

4 Meanwhile, layer the mini buns with salad, if using. Once the burgers are cooked, place on top of the bottom bun and sandwich with the other half.

TOP TIP!
This recipe also works well with turkey mince.

25

CHICKEN GOUJONS

Extra equipment:
- deep fat fryer (see top tip if you don't have one)
- slotted spoon
- paper towels

Ingredients:
- 50 g (2 oz) plain flour
- 3 eggs, beaten
- 125 g (4 1/2 oz) fresh fine breadcrumbs
- 4 boneless and skinless chicken breasts, cut into thin strips

1. Ask an adult to heat a deep fat fryer to 190°C / 375°F.

2. Place the flour, egg and breadcrumbs in three separate bowls.

3. Dip the chicken strips in the flour, then dip into the beaten egg.

4. Then, dip the chicken into the breadcrumbs, making sure the chicken is coated thoroughly.

5. Ask an adult to place the goujons into the deep fat fryer in batches and cook for about 3–4 minutes, until crisp and golden brown and the chicken is completely cooked through. Carefully remove with a slotted spoon and drain onto paper towels.

6. Repeat until all the goujons are cooked and then serve.

TOP TIP!
If you don't have a deep fat fryer, ask an adult to place the goujons in a preheated oven to cook for 10–12 minutes, or until golden brown.

MINI PIZZAS

Extra equipment:
- rolling pin
- large cookie cutters

Ingredients:
- 290 g (10 oz) pizza base mix
- 100 ml (3½ fl.oz) warm water
- tomato purée
- mozzarella cheese
- basil or oregano (optional)
- any topping you like

1 Preheat the oven to 200°C / 400°F / gas mark 6.

2 Empty the pizza base mix into a bowl, add the water, and mix according to the packet instructions.

3 Using a rolling pin, roll the pizza mix dough so it is about 2 cm (1 in.) thick. Use large cookie cutters to cut out shapes.

4 Next, spread a thin layer of the tomato purée onto the base, then add the mozzarella cheese and the herbs.

5 Add the topping of your choice. Why not add a few different toppings, such as brie and cranberry or perhaps a sweet topping like pineapple!

6 Ask an adult to place the mini pizzas into a preheated oven for 10–15 minutes or until they are piping hot and the bases are golden brown.

TOP TIP! Why not arrange the pizza toppings to make funny faces?

VEGETABLE SAMOSAS

TOP TIP!
This recipe is for mild samosas – if you want slightly spicier ones add more chilli!

MAKES 4

Extra equipment:

- pastry brush
- baking tray

Ingredients:

- 1/2 potato
- 1/2 carrot
- 1/2 onion, chopped
- 2 tablespoons oil
- 1/2 red chilli, chopped
- 2 teaspoons garam masala
- 1/2 teaspoon turmeric
- 30 ml (1 fl.oz) water
- 25 g (1 oz) peas (frozen)
- 1/2 teaspoon fresh coriander
- 1 pack filo pastry
- 25 g (1 oz) butter, melted

1 Preheat oven to 200°C / 400°F / gas mark 6.

2 First, ask an adult to peel and dice the potato and carrot into small chunks. Ask an adult to add to a saucepan filled with hot water and boil for 5–8 minutes.

3 Meanwhile, add the onion to a pan and ask an adult to fry in the oil for 4–5 minutes. Add the chilli and spices and cook for a further minute.

4 Drain the potatoes and carrots and add the potatoes, carrots and water to the onion mixture. Continue to fry gently for 5 minutes. Add the peas and coriander and then remove from the heat and allow to cool.

5 Lay 2–3 sheets of filo pastry on the work surface and ask an adult to cut into 10 cm (4 in.) wide strips. Brush with melted butter.

6 Place a tablespoon of filling in the bottom left-hand corner of each filo pastry strip and fold over to make a triangle. Repeat this process for the remaining samosas.

7 Place all of the samosas on a baking tray and brush with melted butter before baking for 10 minutes.

NACHOS & TOMATO SALSA

Extra equipment:
- baking tray

Ingredients:

For the salsa:
- 350 g (12 oz) fresh tomatoes
- 1/2 red onion, chopped
- 1 tablespoon coriander, chopped
- 2 cloves garlic, peeled and crushed

For the nachos:
- 1 large pack of tortilla crisps
- 50 g (2 oz) cheddar cheese, grated
- 1 jalapeno pepper, chopped (optional)

1 Preheat the grill to a medium heat.

To make the salsa:

2 Ask an adult to chop the tomatoes into small pieces, making sure that there are no seeds, and place into a bowl.

3 Place the remaining salsa ingredients into the bowl and mix together well before transferring into a small serving bowl.

To make the nachos:

4 Scatter the tortilla crisps onto a baking tray and sprinkle the cheese and chopped jalapenos over the top so the crisps are evenly covered.

5 Place the tortilla crisps on the baking tray under the preheated grill for 3–4 minutes, until the cheese has melted.

6 Dip your nachos into the salsa and enjoy a taste sensation!

TOP TIP!
Why not add some guacamole and sour cream to your nachos! For some serious spice, add chopped red chillis!

BARBECUE CHICKEN DRUMSTICKS

Extra equipment:

- baking tray

Ingredients:

- 1 teaspoon crushed red pepper
- 2 teaspoons cajun seasoning
- 1 teaspoon chilli powder
- 1/2 teaspoon cornflour
- 6 tablespoons brown sugar
- 100 ml (3 fl.oz) lemon juice
- 500 ml (17 fl.oz) orange juice
- 1 kg (2 lbs, 2 oz) chicken drumsticks
- 1 tablespoon oil

1 Preheat the oven to 180°C / 350°F / gas mark 4.

2 First, make the marinade by combining all of the dry ingredients. Mix together well, then add the lemon juice and orange juice and stir.

3 Place the chicken drumsticks in a deep bowl and cover with the barbecue marinade. Cover and refrigerate for at least 6 hours.

4 Remove the drumsticks from the marinade and place onto a baking tray. Place the marinade in a saucepan, and heat on a low setting until it has thickened.

5 Ask an adult to place the drumsticks in the oven for about 30–35 minutes, turning occasionally and basting with the sauce.

TOP TIP!
Be extra careful when handling raw chicken. Remember to thoroughly wash your hands immediately after you touch it.

HEARTY HOT DOGS

Extra equipment:
- baking tray

Ingredients:
- 8 sausages
- bread rolls of your choice
- salad (optional)
- sauce, to serve (optional)

1 Preheat the oven to 180°C / 350°F / gas mark 4.

2 First, place the sausages onto the baking tray and cook for 20–25 minutes, asking an adult to turn halfway through the cooking time.

3 Meanwhile, ask an adult to open up the bread rolls with a knife.

4 Add any extra filling such as salad and then place a sausage into each roll.

5 Serve them on a plate, leaving sauces on the side (mustard shown).

TOP TIP!
Serve hearty hot dogs with a fun salad face (see page 10).

VEGETABLE CRISPS

Extra equipment:

- swivel peeler or mandolin
- paper towels
- baking tray

Ingredients:

- 2 parsnips
- 2 beetroot
- 2 sweet potatoes
- 2 tablespoons of olive oil
- freshly ground salt and black pepper

1 Preheat the oven to 200°C / 400°F / gas mark 6.

2 Ask an adult to peel all of the vegetables. Using a swivel peeler or mandolin, carefully slice them diagonally into wafer-thin crisps. Spread out on paper towels to remove any excess moisture.

3 Tip all the vegetables into a bowl. Pour over the oil and sprinkle with the salt and black pepper. Toss with your hands to coat evenly.

4 Arrange in a single layer on a baking tray. Roast on the lowest shelf in the oven for 20 minutes, turning halfway through. They are ready when the parsnips and sweet potato are golden brown.

5 Spread out on paper towels until cool and crisp.

TOP TIP!
Veggie crisps taste great with hummus or cheese and chive dips.

32

UNION JACK CUPCAKES

xtra equipment:

- cupcake tray
- Union Jack cupcake cases
- electric whisk (optional)
- icing syringe

ngredients:

- 125 g (4 1/2 oz) self-raising flour
- 125 g (4 1/2 oz) butter, softened
- 125 g (4 1/2 oz) caster sugar
- 2 large eggs
- 2–3 tablespoons milk

For the topping:

- 100 g (4 oz) icing sugar
- 1–2 tablespoons hot water
- food colouring (optional)
- edible Union Jack sugar decorations

1 Preheat the oven to 180°C / 350°F / gas mark 4. Put the cupcake cases in the cupcake tray.

2 Sift the flour into a bowl, followed by the butter. Use the tips of your fingers to rub the butter and flour together until the mixture becomes crumbly. Alternatively, ask an adult to use an electric whisk.

3 Add the sugar and mix it in, then stir in the eggs. Finally, add the milk to make the mixture creamy.

4 Put spoonfuls of the mixture into the cupcake cases. Bake the cupcakes for 10–15 minutes, until they are cooked through and golden brown, then leave them to cool on a wire rack.

5 To make the topping, sift the icing sugar into a bowl and add 1–2 tablespoons of hot water. Mix until you have a smooth, thick paste.

6 If desired, separate the icing into batches and add a few drops of food colouring. Spread the icing onto each cupcake and leave to set.

7 Once set, top each cupcake with a Union Jack sugar decoration and then display.

TOP TIP!
Look out for other Union Jack decorations to continue the theme!

CHOCOLATE BANANAS

Extra equipment:
- tin foil
- baking tray

Ingredients:
- 8 bananas, skin on
- 100 g (4 oz) dark chocolate

1 Preheat the oven to 200°C / 400°F / gas mark 6.

2 Ask an adult to carefully slit each banana lengthways down the centre and through the skin, cutting about halfway through the banana.

3 Break the chocolate into small pieces and place a few pieces into the slit in each banana.

4 Wrap each banana in tin foil and then place onto the baking tray.

5 Place the bananas into the oven and bake for 10–15 minutes, just enough time to allow the bananas to heat and the chocolate to melt.

6 Ask an adult to remove the bananas from the oven, unwrap and enjoy!

TOP TIP!
Serve the bananas with squirty cream for an indulgent treat!

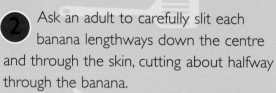

SCONES

Extra equipment:
- baking tray
- sieve
- rolling pin
- 5 cm (2 in.) round pastry cutter

Ingredients:
- 225 g (8 oz) self-raising flour
- 1 teaspoon baking powder
- pinch of salt
- 25 g (1 oz) caster sugar
- 50 g (2 oz) unsalted butter, softened
- 150 ml (5 fl.oz) milk
- 1 egg, beaten
- clotted cream, to serve
- jam, to serve

1. Preheat the oven to 220°C / 425°F / gas mark 7. Grease the baking tray with a little butter.

2. Sift together the flour, baking powder and salt into a bowl. Stir in the sugar.

3. Add the butter and rub it into the flour mixture until it resembles fine breadcrumbs.

4. Add the milk, a little at a time, until it becomes a smooth dough.

5. Lightly flour the work surface and then roll out the dough until it is about 2 cm (3/4 in.) thick.

6. Use the pastry cutter to cut the dough into round scones. Re-roll any dough that is left over and cut out more scones. Place onto the baking tray.

7. Brush the tops of the scones with the beaten egg. Ask an adult to place in the oven and bake for 10–12 minutes, or until golden brown.

8. Serve with clotted cream and jam.

TOP TIP!
Why not try making fruit scones by adding 50 g (2 oz) raisins or sultanas to the dry ingredients?

CRISPY SQUARES

Extra equipment:
- 22 x 33 cm (9 x 13 in) baking tin
- greaseproof paper
- forks, to serve

Ingredients:
- 50 g (2 oz) butter
- 1 teaspoon vanilla extract
- 200 g (7 oz) marshmallows
- 100 g (4 oz) crisped rice cereal

1 Wipe around the sides and bottom of the baking tin with a little oil or butter on a paper towel.

2 In a large saucepan, ask an adult to melt the butter over a low heat. Add the vanilla extract and melt the marshmallows into the butter, stirring all the time.

3 Add the rice cereal when the marshmallows have melted and stir until the cereal is coated. Quickly pour into the tin. Use a sheet of greaseproof paper to press the mixture down flat and evenly into the tin.

4 Let the crispies set for 2 to 3 hours. Cut into squares and insert forks into them for easy eating!

TOP TIP! Why not add sweets or chocolate buttons along with the crisped cereal?

36

FAIRY CAKES

Extra equipment:
- cupcake cases
- cupcake tray

Ingredients:
- 100 g (4 oz) butter
- 100 g (4 oz) caster sugar
- 2 eggs
- 100 g (4 oz) self-raising flour

For the topping:
- 80 g (3 oz) butter
- 150 g (5 oz) icing sugar
- 1–2 tablespoons milk

1 Preheat the oven to 180°C / 350°F / gas mark 4. Put the cupcake cases into the cupcake tray.

2 Put the butter and sugar into a mixing bowl. Use a wooden spoon to beat them together until the mixture is fluffy and very pale in colour. Beat in the eggs, one at a time, adding a tablespoon of flour with each one. Sift the rest of the flour into the bowl. Use a tablespoon to mix the ingredients gently. This will make sure your mixture stays nice and fluffy.

3 Use a teaspoon to transfer equal amounts of the mixture to the cupcake cases. Bake the cakes for 20–25 minutes or until they are well risen and golden brown. Leave them to cool on a wire rack.

4 To make the wings, cut a slice from the top of each cake. Now cut each slice in half.

5 To make the buttercream topping, use a wooden spoon or an electric mixer to beat the butter in a large bowl until it is soft. Sift half of the icing sugar into the bowl, and then beat it with the butter until the mixture is smooth. Then, sift the rest of the icing sugar into the bowl and add one tablespoon of milk. Beat the mixture until it is smooth and creamy.

6 Place a little buttercream icing on top of each cake. Now, gently push two of the halved slices into the icing on each cake at an angle to form pretty wings.

TOP TIP!
Be extra careful when placing the fiddly wings!

CINNAMON DOUGHNUTS

Extra equipment:
- rolling pin

Ingredients:
- 2 eggs
- 100 g (3 ½ oz) caster sugar
- 1 vanilla pod, seeds scraped out
- 100 ml (3 ½ fl.oz) crème fraîche
- 375 g (13 ½ oz) plain flour, plus extra for dusting
- pinch salt
- 1 tablespoon baking powder
- 1 teaspoon bicarbonate of soda
- vegetable oil, for deep frying
- 2 teaspoons cinnamon, to decorate
- 3 tablespoons caster sugar, to decorate

1 In a bowl, beat the eggs, sugar and vanilla seeds for five minutes, then stir in the crème fraîche.

2 Sift in the flour, salt, baking powder and bicarbonate of soda and mix well. Knead on a floured surface for 2–3 minutes until a smooth dough forms.

3 Roll out the dough to about 5 mm (½ in.) thick and cut out 7.5 cm (3 in.) circles. Make a small hole in the centre of each doughnut.

4 Ask an adult to half-fill a large saucepan with vegetable oil and heat until a small cube of bread turns golden in 30 seconds. **Do not leave hot oil unattended.**

5 Ask an adult to fry the doughnuts in the oil for 3–4 minutes, or until golden brown. Do this in batches to avoid over-crowding the pan.

6 In a small bowl mix the cinnamon and caster sugar.

7 Once the doughnuts have cooled slightly, roll each in the sugar mix until well covered.

TOP TIP! For filled doughnuts, shape into circles and fry. Once cooked, pipe in custard or jam!

BERRY ICE POPS

Extra equipment:
- blender
- ice lolly moulds

Ingredients:
- 225 g (8 oz) fresh mixed berries
- 50 g (2 oz) icing sugar
- 2 tablespoons clear honey
- 2 tablespoons lemon juice
- 900 ml (1 1/2 pt) natural yogurt

1 Put all of the ingredients in a blender, reserving a few of the smaller berries for later. Ask an adult to process the mixture until smooth. (If you have not got a blender, place the ingredients into a bowl and ask an adult to blend the mixture with a hand-held electric whisk.)

2 Now add the reserved smaller berries to the mixture and pour into the lolly moulds. Place the moulds into a freezer.

3 When the mixture has partially frozen, rotate the moulds – this way the larger pieces of fruit won't clump together. Leave them to set for at least 4 hours, until solid.

4 Remove the lollies from the freezer and let them stand at room temperature for 5 minutes. Then, remove from the moulds and enjoy!

TOP TIP!
Any leftover mixture can be made into a smoothie! Just blitz it in a blender with some more yogurt and milk if it's too thick!

PARTY CAKES

MAKES 12

Extra equipment:
- cupcake cases
- cupcake tray
- piping bag

Ingredients:
- 125 g (4 1/2 oz) self-raising flour
- 125 g (4 1/2 oz) butter, softened
- 125 g (4 1/2 oz) caster sugar
- 2 large eggs
- a few drops of vanilla extract
- 2–3 tablespoons milk

For the topping:
- whipped cream
- sugar sprinkles

1 Preheat the oven to 180°C / 350°F / gas mark 4.

2 Sift the flour into a bowl, followed by the butter. Use the tips of your fingers to rub the butter and flour together until the mixture becomes crumbly. Alternatively, ask an adult to use an electric whisk.

3 Add the sugar and mix it in, then stir in the eggs. Finally, add the vanilla extract and milk to make the mixture creamy.

4 Put spoonfuls of the mixture into the cupcake cases. Bake the cupcakes for 10–15 minutes, until they are golden brown, then leave them to cool on a wire rack.

5 Once cool, place the whipped cream into a piping bag and pipe onto the top of the cupcakes.

6 Finish with sugar sprinkles.

TOP TIP! For a bit of celebratory sparkle, try adding edible glitter as an alternative decoration!

COCONUT CUPCAKES

Extra equipment:
- cupcake cases
- cupcake tray

Ingredients:
- 225 g (8 oz) self-raising flour
- 75 g (3 oz) butter
- 75 g (3 oz) caster sugar
- 1 egg
- 75–100 ml (2–4 fl.oz) milk

For the topping:
- whipped cream
- pink coconut ice, grated

1 Preheat the oven to 180°C / 350°F / gas mark 4.

2 Sift the flour into a bowl, followed by the butter. Use the tips of your fingers to rub the butter and flour together until the mixture becomes crumbly.

3 Add the sugar and stir in the egg.

4 Finally, add enough milk to make the mixture creamy.

5 Put spoonfuls of the mixture into the cupcake cases. Bake the cupcakes for 10–15 minutes, then leave them to cool on a wire rack.

6 Decorate them with a generous swirl of freshly whipped cream and cover with grated pink coconut ice.

TOP TIP!
Place a plate underneath each cupcake whilst you sprinkle the coconut ice.

VANILLA ICE CREAM

Extra equipment:

• electric whisk

• ice cream maker (optional)

Ingredients:

• 500 ml (17 fl.oz) double cream

• 1 vanilla pod, split

• 100 g (4 oz) caster sugar

• 150 ml (5 fl.oz) water

• 4 egg yolks

• strawberries, to decorate

• mint leaves, to decorate

1 Ask an adult to heat the cream in a saucepan so that it almost boils and then remove from the heat. Add the split vanilla pod and leave it until the cream is completely cool.

2 Scrape the tiny seeds from the vanilla pod into the cream and remove the pod casing.

3 Dissolve the sugar in the water over a low heat. Then, ask an adult to turn up the heat and boil the mixture to create a light syrup. Leave the syrup mixture to cool for 1 minute.

4 Place the egg yolks in a bowl and ask an adult to whisk them using an electric whisk, slowly adding the hot syrup.

5 Continue to whisk until the mixture thickens and is mousse-like. Then, whisk in the cream and pour into an ice cream maker and churn until frozen. Alternatively, if you don't have an ice cream maker you can freeze your ice cream in a plastic tub in the freezer. You will need to stir the mixture every hour to break up any ice.

6 Serve your ice cream when it's frozen.

TOP TIP! Serve your vanilla ice cream with strawberries and a mint leaf garnish.

LEMON POPPY MUFFINS

Extra equipment:
- muffin cases
- muffin baking tray

Ingredients:
- 375 g (13 oz) plain flour
- 1 tablespoon baking powder
- 1/2 teaspoon bicarbonate of soda
- 2 tablespoons poppy seeds
- 140 g (5 oz) unsalted butter
- 200 g (7 oz) sugar
- 2 eggs
- 1 tablespoon lemon zest
- 350 ml (12 fl.oz) plain yogurt

For the topping:
- 2 tablespoons fresh lemon juice
- 120 g (4 oz) icing sugar

1 Preheat the oven to 190°C / 375°F / gas mark 5. Put the cases in the muffin baking tray.

2 Ask an adult to help you grate a lemon, but be careful not to grate any of the white pith. Cut the lemon in half and squeeze the juice into a bowl and set aside.

3 Mix together the flour, baking powder, bicarbonate of soda and poppy seeds, and set aside.

4 In a large mixing bowl, cream the butter and sugar together, beating until fluffy. Beat in the eggs one at a time. Add the lemon zest and then beat in half of the dry ingredients and half of the yogurt.

5 Next, beat in the remaining dry ingredients followed by the remaining yogurt.

6 Spoon the mixture into the muffin cases, and bake the muffins for 25–30 minutes, or until they are golden brown.

7 For the icing, put the icing sugar into a bowl with the lemon juice. Mix together well, until it forms a smooth paste.

8 While the muffins are still warm, spoon a little of the icing over each one. Leave to cool completely.

JAMMY TARTS

Extra equipment:
- tart tray
- cookie cutters

Ingredients:
- butter, for greasing
- 250 g (9 oz) ready-made sweet shortcrust pastry
- plain flour, for dusting

For the filling:
- 450 g (1 lb) strawberries, hulls removed
- 450 g (1 lb) golden caster sugar
- 1 tablespoon vanilla extract
- mint leaves, to serve

1 Preheat the oven to 180°C / 350°F / gas mark 4. Grease the tart tray with butter.

2 On a lightly floured surface, roll out the shortcrust pastry to 1/2 cm (1/4 in.).

3 Use a cookie cutter to cut discs from the pastry that are slightly bigger than the holes in the tart tray. Press a pastry disc into each of the holes.

4 Put the strawberries, sugar and vanilla extract into a saucepan and ask an adult to bring the mixture to a simmer. Simmer for 5–8 minutes, or until the strawberries start to break down. Set the mixture aside to cool slightly.

5 Once the filling has cooled slightly, spoon it into the centre of each pastry case.

6 Roll out the remaining shortcrust pastry to 1/2 cm (1/4 in.) and cut into thin strips. Criss-cross the strips on top of each tart.

7 Ask an adult to put the tarts in the oven and bake for 10–12 minutes, or until the pastry is golden-brown. Remove the tarts from the oven and put them on a wire rack to cool.

8 Once cool, garnish with mint leaves and enjoy!

44

CAKE POPS

Extra equipment:
- 8 lollipop sticks
- baking tray
- greaseproof paper

Ingredients:
- 100 g (3 ½ oz) dark chocolate
- 125 g (4 ½ oz) fruit cake
- 125 g (4 ½ oz) Madeira cake
- 2 tablespoons desiccated coconut
- 2 tablespoons chopped hazelnuts

To decorate:
- 300 g (10 ½ oz) white chocolate

1 Ask an adult to melt the dark chocolate in a bowl set over a pan of simmering water, making sure the base of the bowl doesn't touch the water.

2 Crumble the fruit cake and Madeira cake into a bowl, then stir in the melted chocolate, desiccated coconut and hazelnuts until well combined.

3 Roll golf-ball-sized pieces of the mixture into balls. Stick a wooden stick into each ball and set aside in the fridge for 20–30 minutes, or until firm.

4 Then, ask an adult to melt the white chocolate in a bowl set over a pan of simmering water, making sure the base of the bowl doesn't touch the water.

5 Line the baking tray with greaseproof paper.

6 Remove the balls from the fridge. Dip each in the melted chocolate, making sure they are all completely coated.

7 Place onto the baking tray and set aside in the refrigerator for 20–30 minutes, or until the chocolate has set.

TOP TIP! This recipe works just as well with a dark or milk chocolate coating!

45

PINEAPPLE PUNCH

Extra equipment:
- blender

Ingredients:
- 1 pineapple
- 375 ml (12 fl.oz) milk
- 375 ml (12 fl.oz) pineapple yogurt
- 3 scoops vanilla ice cream (see home-made recipe on p.42 or use shop-bought)

1 Ask an adult to prepare the pineapple. First, remove the leafy top and the base. Then, slice the skin away, from top to bottom. Cut the pineapple in half, then into thick wedges. Remove the central core and then chop the wedges into small pieces.

2 Place all of the ingredients into a blender, reserving slices of pineapple for decoration, and ask an adult to blend until smooth. (If you have not got a blender, place the ingredients into a bowl and ask an adult to blend the mixture with a hand-held whisk.)

3 Pour into two glasses, and decorate with pineapple slices.

4 Serve immediately.

TOP TIP! Try making a whole jug of pineapple punch and leaving it on the table so everyone can help themselves!

CHOCOLATE ICE CREAM

Extra equipment:
- electric whisk
- ice cream maker (optional)

Ingredients:
- 300 g (10 oz) dark chocolate, finely chopped
- 240 ml (8 fl.oz) milk
- 240 ml (8 fl.oz) double cream
- 175 g (6 oz) caster sugar
- 4 large egg yolks
- 150 ml (5 fl.oz) water

1 First, tip 200 g (7 oz) of dark chocolate into a heatproof bowl, reserving the rest to add to the ice cream later. Heat the milk, double cream and 25 g (1 oz) of caster sugar in a saucepan, then pour over the chocolate and stir until dissolved. Leave on one side until cool.

2 Ask an adult to whisk the egg yolks with an electric whisk and add this to the cooled chocolate cream mixture.

3 Next, place 150 g (5 oz) of sugar in a saucepan and add 150 ml (5 fl.oz) of water. Dissolve the sugar over a medium heat, stirring occasionally. Then, bring to a boil and cook for 5 minutes.

4 Ask an adult to pour the hot sugar syrup into the chocolate cream mixture, in a thin steady stream, whilst you whisk. Continue whisking until the mixture has thickened and is similar to a mousse – this should take about 5 minutes.

5 Add the extra chocolate and stir to blend everything together. Pour into an ice cream maker and churn until frozen. Alternatively, you could freeze the mixture in a tub, stirring it every hour to break up any ice and ensure that the chocolate is evenly mixed in.

6 Once it is frozen, scoop and serve!

TOP TIP! Why not serve the ice cream in wafer cones!

CHOCOLATE FUDGE BROWNIES

Extra equipment:
- 20 cm (8 in.) square cake tin
- baking parchment

Ingredients:
- 2 eggs
- 225 g (8 oz) caster sugar
- 100 g (4 oz) butter
- 3 tablespoons cocoa powder
- 100 g (4 oz) self-raising flour
- 50 g (2 oz) pecans, chopped

For the topping:
- 50 g (2 oz) butter
- 1 tablespoon milk
- 100 g (4 oz) icing sugar
- 2 tablespoons cocoa powder
- pecan or walnut halves, to decorate

1 Preheat the oven to 180°C / 350°F / gas mark 4.

2 Beat the eggs and the sugar together in a bowl, until light and fluffy.

3 Ask an adult to melt the butter in the microwave (5 seconds max) and beat in the cocoa powder before adding to the eggs and sugar.

4 Sift the self-raising flour and fold into the main mixture with the chopped pecans.

5 Grease a 20 cm (8 in.) square cake tin with butter, then line it with baking parchment. Pour in the mixture and bake in the oven for 40–45 minutes.

6 For the topping, melt the butter in a small pan and add the milk. Remove from the heat, then beat in the icing sugar and cocoa powder.

7 Spread icing over the cooked brownies and decorate with pecans or walnut halves. Cut into squares when the topping is firm.

TOP TIP! If you don't like nuts, try mixing in some chocolate chips or raisins!

COLOURFUL CUPCAKES

xtra equipment:
- cupcake cases
- cupcake tray
- rolling pin
- cookie cutters

ngredients:
- 225 g (8 oz) self-raising flour
- 80 g (3 oz) butter
- 80 g (3 oz) caster sugar
- 1 egg
- 75–100 ml (3–4 fl.oz) milk

or the topping:
- ready-to-roll icing
- food colouring

1 Preheat the oven to 180°C / 350°F / gas mark 4. Put the cupcake cases into the cupcake tray.

2 Sift the flour into a bowl, followed by the butter. Use your fingertips to rub the butter and flour together until the mixture becomes crumbly.

3 Add the sugar and mix it in, then stir in the egg. Finally, add enough milk to make the mixture creamy.

4 Put spoonfuls of the mixture into the cupcake cases. Bake the cupcakes for 10–15 minutes, until they are golden brown, then leave them to cool.

5 For the decorative topping, knead a couple of drops of food colouring into some of the icing. When the colour is even, roll out the icing and cut out shapes, either with a cookie cutter or ask an adult to use a sharp knife. Lay the different shapes over the tops of the cupcakes.

6 Repeat the process, with different food colourings and icing shapes.

TOP TIP!
Experiment with different shapes and colours. Try to make each cupcake look different!

ICED BISCUITS

Extra equipment:
- baking tray
- baking paper
- sieve
- rolling pin
- cookie cutters
- palette knife

Ingredients:
- 100 g (4 oz) butter
- 100 g (4 oz) caster sugar
- 1 egg
- 1 teaspoon vanilla extract
- 275 g (10 oz) plain flour

For the icing:
- 400 g (14 oz) icing sugar
- 3–4 tablespoons water
- food colouring (optional)
- assorted sugar sprinkles, sweets, edible glitter (optional)

1. Preheat the oven to 190°C / 375°F / gas mark 5. Line the baking tray with baking paper.

2. Cream the butter and sugar together in a bowl until light and fluffy. Add the egg and vanilla extract, a little at a time, and mix well.

3. Sift the flour into the creamed mixture and, using your hands, create a smooth, firm dough. Refrigerate the mixture for 15 minutes.

4. Roll the dough out on a floured surface until it is 1 cm (1/2 in.) thick. Using either a sharp knife or cookie cutters, cut out shapes from the dough and transfer to the baking tray.

5. Bake the cookies in the oven for 8–10 minutes, or until golden brown then transfer to a wire rack to cool.

6. To make the icing, sift the icing sugar into a bowl and add enough water to make a smooth, thick paste. Add one or two drops of food colouring if you wish.

7. Use the palette knife to spread the icing over the cookies and leave to set. Top with sugar sprinkles, sweets or edible glitter.

TOP TIP! Separate the icing into batches and add different food colouring to each for rainbow-coloured biscuits!

BANANA MILKSHAKE

Extra equipment:
* blender

Ingredients:
* 2 bananas
* 350 ml (12 fl.oz) coconut milk
* a large dash of maple syrup
* 4 ice cubes, crushed

1 Peel the banana and ask an adult to slice it into small chunks.

2 Next, place all of the ingredients in a blender and blend until smooth. (If you have not got a blender, place the ingredients into a bowl and ask an adult to blend the mixture with a hand-held whisk.)

3 Pour into two glasses.

4 Drink immediately.

TOP TIP! Double the ingredients to make double the milkshake!

51

ROCKY ROAD

Extra equipment:
- 23 cm (9 in.) square baking tin
- clean freezer bag
- rolling pin
- spatula

Ingredients:
- 125 g (4 1/2 oz) butter, softened
- 300 g (10 1/2 oz) dark chocolate, broken into pieces
- 45 ml (1 1/2 fl.oz) golden syrup
- 200 g (7 oz) digestive biscuits
- 100 g (3 1/2 oz) mini marshmallows
- 50 g (1 3/4 oz) dried cranberries
- 50 g (1 3/4 oz) toasted pistachios, chopped
- 50 g (1 3/4 oz) milk chocolate chunks

1 Grease the baking tin with a little butter. Ask an adult to melt the butter, chocolate and golden syrup in a saucepan. When melted, mix well.

2 Put the biscuits into a freezer bag and break up with a rolling pin until you have a mixture of fine crumbs and small pieces.

3 Mix the biscuit pieces into the melted chocolate mixture in the saucepan. Then add the marshmallows, cranberries and chopped pistachios.

4 Tip into the baking tin and flatten with a spatula. Sprinkle the milk chocolate chunks over the top.

5 Refrigerate for about 2 hours, or preferably overnight.

6 To serve, cut into 25 squares. Keep refrigerated.

TOP TIP! If you don't like marshmallows, add 100 g (3 1/2 oz) raisins in step 3.

STRAWBERRY ICE CREAM

Extra equipment:

• blender

• sieve

• ice cream maker (optional)

Ingredients:

• 350 g (12 oz) strawberries, hulled and roughly chopped

• 100 g (4 oz) caster sugar

• 2 egg yolks

• 300 ml (10 fl.oz) double cream

• wafer stick, to decorate

1 Ask an adult to purée the strawberries in a blender (reserving a couple for decoration), then sieve to remove any bits.

2 Put the caster sugar and egg yolks together in a bowl and whisk until thick.

3 Bring the cream to the boil in a saucepan and then gradually whisk it into the egg yolk mixture.

4 Pour the cream / egg yolk mixture back into the pan and cook over a low heat for 5 minutes, or until the mixture sticks to the back of a wooden spoon.

5 Strain the mixture into a bowl and add the strawberry purée.

6 Pour the mixture into an ice cream maker and churn until frozen. Alternatively, if you don't have an ice cream maker you can freeze your ice cream in a plastic tub in the freezer. You will need to stir the mixture every hour to break up any ice.

7 Serve your ice cream when it's frozen.

TOP TIP! Serve with fresh strawberries and a wafer stick to give your ice cream the 'wow' factor!

CARAMEL APPLES

Extra equipment:
- baking tray
- baking paper
- 6 wooden sticks

Ingredients:
- 6 small apples
- 225 g (8 oz) granulated sugar
- 110 ml (4 fl.oz) water
- 30 g (1 oz) butter
- 2 tablespoons golden syrup
- 4 tablespoons mixed nuts, finely chopped (optional)

1 Line the baking tray with baking paper.

2 Push the wooden sticks halfway into each apple at the stalk end.

3 Ask an adult to dissolve the sugar and water in a thick-bottomed pan over a gentle heat.

4 Add the butter and syrup to the mixture and ask an adult to bring to the boil. Reduce the heat and simmer for 12–15 minutes, or until the caramel is a deep, amber colour. Don't stir the caramel at this stage or it will become grainy.

5 Remove the pan from the heat and allow to cool slightly.

6 Carefully dip each apple into the caramel, making sure it is well coated, then place on the baking tray to cool and harden. Dip the apples into the chopped nuts before allowing to cool completely (optional).

TOP TIP!
Experiment with the toppings – try melted chocolate instead!

CRANBERRY COOLER

Extra equipment:
- blender

Ingredients:
- 3 handfuls strawberries
- 1 small banana
- 150 ml (5 fl.oz) cranberry juice
- 225 ml (7 ½ fl.oz) natural yogurt
- handful of cranberries
- 8 ice cubes, crushed

1 Wash and prepare the fruit to start with. Ask an adult to chop the strawberries and slice the banana into small pieces.

2 Place all of the ingredients in a blender and ask an adult to blend until smooth. (If you have not got a blender, place the ingredients into a bowl and ask an adult to blend the mixture with a hand-held whisk.)

3 Pour into two glasses.

4 Top with a handful of cranberries, then drink immediately.

TOP TIP! Experiment with your choice of fruit topping. Blackcurrants are especially good!

CELEBRATORY COOKIES

Extra equipment:
- baking tray
- baking paper
- rolling pin
- shaped cookie cutters

Ingredients:
- 125 g (4 oz) butter, softened
- 175 g (6 oz) caster sugar
- 1 egg
- 1 tablespoon golden syrup
- 250 g (9 oz) plain flour
- 1/2 teaspoon baking powder
- 2 teaspoons ground ginger

To decorate:
- icing sugar, for dusting
- assorted sweets

1 Preheat the oven to 180°C / 350°F / gas mark 4. Line the baking tray with baking paper.

2 Cream the butter and sugar together in a bowl until light and fluffy.

3 Lightly beat the egg and stir into the butter mixture with the golden syrup.

4 Mix in the flour, baking powder and ground ginger. Stir until well combined.

5 Roll out the mixture until it is about 1/2 cm (1/4 in.) thick. Use the cookie cutters to cut out the cookies then place onto the baking tray. Re-roll any leftover mixture and cut again.

6 Ask an adult to place the cookies into the oven and bake for 8–10 minutes, or until golden-brown.

7 Lay out on a wire rack and dust generously with icing sugar while the cookies are still warm, so the icing sugar melts. To finish, decorate the cookies with your favourite sweets before the icing sugar sets.

TOP TIP!
If you have any cookies left over, wrap the rest up so your neighbours can take them home to enjoy the next day!

CHOCOLATE OAT CRUNCHIES

Extra equipment:
• baking tray
• round cookie cutter

Ingredients:
• 100 g (4 oz) soft margarine
• 75 g (3 oz) demerara sugar
• 100 g (4 oz) plain wholemeal flour
• 100 g (4 oz) porridge oats
• 50 g (2 oz) chocolate chips

1. Preheat the oven to 180°C / 350°F / gas mark 4.

2. Use a paper towel to grease the baking tray with a little soft margarine.

3. Put the margarine and sugar into a bowl and mix them together with a wooden spoon.

4. Add the flour, oats and chocolate chips to the bowl. Mix everything together, using a spoon and then your hands, to make a soft dough.

5. Put the dough onto a floured surface and gently press it out.

6. Cut out circles of dough and put them onto the baking tray.

7. Bake the crunchies in the oven for 12–15 minutes, until they are golden brown. Place them onto a wire rack to cool.

TOP TIP!
Try adding chopped nuts instead of chocolate chips for extra crunch!

HOMEMADE LEMONADE

Extra equipment:

• heatproof jug

• sieve

Ingredients:

• 4 unwaxed lemons, washed

• 100 g (4 oz) caster sugar

• 570 ml (1 pt) boiling water

• 400 ml (13 ½ fl.oz) chilled
  still water

• ice, crushed

1 Ask an adult to grate the zest from the lemons, leaving as much white pith behind as possible.

2 Half the lemons, then squeeze the juice into a large heatproof jug. Also, place the zest and sugar into the jug.

3 Pour in 570 ml (1 pt) of boiling water and stir until the sugar has dissolved. Cover, and leave to cool completely.

4 Now, strain the mixture into a serving jug, and discard the zest. Dilute with the chilled water and sweeten with extra sugar to taste.

5 Serve decorated with lemon slices and crushed ice.

TOP TIP!
Add a pinch of lime zest as well for an added citrus kick!

COLOURFUL ICE CUBES

Extra equipment:
• ice cube tray

Ingredients:
• 350 ml (12 fl.oz) water
• splash of fruit cordial or a few drops of food colouring

1 Ask an adult to boil a kettle and then let it cool. Pour the cooled water into the ice cube tray. (Ice made from boiled water turns out clear, rather than cloudy.)

2 Next, add either a splash of fruit cordial to each cube or a drop of food colouring to make the cubes colourful.

3 Place the ice cube tray into a freezer and let the cubes set for at least 4 hours, until solid.

4 Remove the ice cubes from the tray and enjoy, either on their own or in a cool drink!

TOP TIP!
Alternate with different colours to create a rainbow of ice cubes!

JELLY BEAN JAM CUPCAKES

Extra equipment:
- cupcake cases
- cupcake tray

Ingredients:
- 125 g (4 ½ oz) self-raising flour
- 125 g (4 ½ oz) butter, softened
- 125 g (4 ½ oz) caster sugar
- 2 large eggs
- 2–3 tablespoons milk
- 100 g (4 oz) fruit jam

For the topping:
- 100 g (4 oz) icing sugar
- 1–2 tablespoons hot water
- a few drops of pink food colouring
- 12 jelly beans

1 Preheat the oven to 180°C / 350°F / gas mark 4. Put the cupcake cases into the cupcake tray.

2 Sift the flour into a bowl, followed by the butter. Use the tips of your fingers to rub the butter and flour together until the mixture becomes crumbly. Alternatively, ask an adult to use an electric whisk.

3 Add the sugar and mix it in, then stir in the eggs. Finally, add the milk to make the mixture creamy.

4 Put spoonfuls of the mixture into the cupcake cases, filling them halfway. Drop a teaspoonful of jam on top of the mixture and then cover with the remaining mixture.

5 Bake the cupcakes for 10–15 minutes, until they are golden brown, then leave them to cool on a wire rack.

6 To make the topping, sift the icing sugar into a bowl and add 1–2 tablespoons of hot water. Mix until you have a thick paste.

7 Add one or two drops of pink food colouring. Once well mixed, spoon the icing onto each cupcake and top with a jelly bean.

TOP TIP! Add more than one jelly bean to each cupcake if you like!

MINI COOKIE SANDWICHES

Extra equipment:
- 2 baking trays
- baking paper

Ingredients:
- 150 g (5 oz) plain flour
- 150 g (5 oz) ground almonds
- 150 g (5 oz) caster sugar
- 125 g (4 ½ oz) butter
- 1 teaspoon vanilla essence
- 2-3 teaspoons water

For the filling:
- 200 g (7 oz) dark chocolate, chopped

1 Preheat the oven to 150°C / 300°F / gas mark 2. Line two baking trays with baking paper.

2 In a large bowl, mix together the flour, ground almonds and sugar. Then, rub in the butter with your fingertips until it looks crumbly. Add the vanilla essence and sufficient water to just bind the ingredients, forming a stiff dough. Work the dough lightly for two to three minutes.

3 Using the palms of your hands, form small amounts of dough into balls the size of cherries. Place them on a baking tray and flatten each one slightly.

4 Cook them in the centre of the oven for 15–20 minutes until golden brown.

5 Allow them to cool on a wire rack.

6 Ask an adult to place a heatproof bowl over a bowl of gently simmering water and add the chopped chocolate. Heat until the chocolate has just melted, stirring gently. Be careful not to overheat.

7 Allow the chocolate to cool a little then, using a teaspoon, place a little of the melted chocolate onto one of the biscuits. Take another of the biscuits and press them together. Continue making cookie 'sandwiches' until they have been used up.

TOP TIP!
Allow the chocolate to cool completely before serving these delicious cookies!

CHOCOLATE-CHIP COOKIES

Extra equipment:
• baking tray
• sieve

Ingredients:
• 125 g (4 ½ oz) butter
• 100 g (4 oz) caster sugar
• 75 g (3 oz) brown sugar
• 1 egg
• a few drops of vanilla extract
• 150 g (5 oz) plain flour
• ½ teaspoon baking powder
• 50 g (2 oz) chocolate chips

1. Preheat the oven to 180°C / 350°F / gas mark 4.

2. Use a paper towel to grease the baking tray with a little butter.

3. Put the butter and both sugars into a large bowl and mix them together with a wooden spoon until they are light and fluffy.

4. Add the egg and the vanilla extract and beat well.

5. Sift the plain flour and baking powder into the bowl. Stir them into the mixture, then add the chocolate chips.

6. Put 8–10 teaspoons of the mixture onto the greased tray (you will probably have enough mixture for two batches). Bake the cookies for 15–20 minutes or until golden brown.

7. Leave them to cool for 2–3 minutes before lifting them onto a wire rack to cool completely.

TOP TIP!
Don't be afraid to experiment with the recipe – add nuts, sweets or more chocolate!

CROWN COOKIES

Extra equipment:
- baking tray
- baking paper
- sieve
- rolling pin
- crown-shaped cookie cutter

Ingredients:
- 100 g (4 oz) butter, softened
- 100 g (4 oz) caster sugar
- 1 egg
- 1 teaspoon vanilla extract
- 275 g (10 oz) plain flour

For the topping:
- red ready-to-roll icing
- yellow ready-to-roll icing
- small and large edible silver balls

1 Preheat the oven to 190°C / 375°F / gas mark 5. Line the baking tray with baking paper.

2 Cream the butter and sugar together until the mixture is light and fluffy. Add the egg and vanilla extract, a little at a time, and mix well.

3 Sift the flour into the creamed mixture and, using your hands, create a smooth, firm dough. Refrigerate the mixture for 15 minutes.

4 Roll the dough out on a floured surface until it is 1/2 cm (1/4 in.) thick. Use the crown-shaped cookie cutter, or ask an adult to use a sharp knife, to cut out shapes from the dough. Transfer to the baking tray.

5 Bake the cookies in the oven for 8–10 minutes, or until golden brown, then transfer to a wire rack to cool.

6 Thinly roll out the red ready-to-roll icing. Carefully cut out a shape to fit the inside of the crown and place one on each cookie.

7 Next, roll out the yellow ready-to-roll icing. Use the crown-shaped cookie cutter to cut out icing crowns. Ask an adult to cut spaces in the icing for the red to show through, and carefully place on the cookies. Gently press down to hold.

8 Finally, use small and large edible silver balls to decorate.

TOP TIP! Experiment with the decoration — try recreating the crown jewels!

INDEX OF RECIPES